THE CHRISTMAS TREE EFFECT

A Guide to Effectively Preaching the Gospel

Clark Dunkle

ISBN 978-1-0980-0643-3 (paperback)
ISBN 978-1-0980-0644-0 (digital)

Copyright © 2019 by Clark Dunkle

All rights reserved. No part of this publication may be reproduced, distributed, or transmitted in any form or by any means, including photocopying, recording, or other electronic or mechanical methods without the prior written permission of the publisher. For permission requests, solicit the publisher via the address below.

Christian Faith Publishing, Inc.
832 Park Avenue
Meadville, PA 16335
www.christianfaithpublishing.com

Printed in the United States of America

To Teresa:

What can I say? You are my wife, partner and most of all my best friend. Your beauty and love know no bounds. Even though I have given you many opportunities to walk away, you have given them all up and for that I am eternally grateful. Without your unconditional love and support this book as well as my ministry would never have been possible.

To Ted:

My brother, you have made the two most important introductions in my life. Most importantly, to the Lord Jesus Christ whose love makes everything possible and to Brennan Manning, who unveiled to me the unconditional love of God thorough his many books.

To Cheryl:

My sister, without you I am sure that the chapter of my life entitled 2011 would have a very different ending. Your strength and integrity during Mother's final days was phenomenal. Personally, I will be forever grateful for your guidance and support in the face of my prostate cancer diagnosis.

Chapter 1

Two Thousand Eleven

I suppose anyone, when they take the time to reminisce about their life, will be able to point to one year more than others which have profoundly affected the rest of their lives. As I enter the beginning of my sixth decade of life, you would think years—such as the one where I lost my father less than two weeks from beginning my freshman year in college, the year that I met my wife Teresa, the year that we were married, and the years that my daughter and granddaughters were born—would be worthy candidates. Surely the two years spent in federal incarceration allowing God to transform a thoroughly broken man into a minister of the Gospel of grace would shoot to the very top of the list, but that is not the case.

The events and the aftereffects of the roller-coaster year (in actuality seven months) of 2011 not only shook my life to the core but also continue to have an effect on my everyday life. They range from the depth of sorrow to the joy of new life, the grip of fear, the facing of my own mortality, the excitement of being in the presence of one of the most admired and anointed Christian musical artists of our time, and the revelation from God that continue to be dynamically revealed to me. I continued to preach and teach until this very day.

These events did not just intersect but actually intertwined to culminate into a revelation that I believe is crucial to be able to do what Jesus asked us to do, and that is to *simply* preach the Gospel to *every* creature.

Now as I sit here writing this account of these events in 2011, it is seven years later, and it has become extremely clear to me now that it is time to broaden the audience with the revelation that God revealed to me out of the confluence of the events which I will reveal in this book. Matthew 24:5–12 (KJV) says,

> "For many shall come in my name, saying, I am Christ; and shall deceive many. And ye shall hear of wars and rumours of wars: see that ye be not troubled: for all these things must come to pass, but the end is not yet. For nation shall rise against nation, and kingdom against kingdom: and there shall be famines, and pestilences, and earthquakes, in divers places. All these are the beginning of sorrows. Then shall they deliver you up to be afflicted and shall kill you: and ye shall be hated of all nations for my name's sake. And then shall many be offended, and shall betray one another, and shall hate one another. And many false prophets shall rise and shall deceive many. And because iniquity shall abound, the love of many shall wax cold. But he that shall endure unto the end, the same shall be saved. And this gospel of the kingdom shall be preached in all the world for a witness unto all nations; and then shall the end come."

Down through the ages, even until today, I believe that the focus has been misplaced in this series of verses.

THE CHRISTMAS TREE EFFECT

When discussing the impending return of Jesus Christ, the debate has largely been about the first part. Oh, we are quick to point out the wars and rumors of wars part and the many disasters and miseries that we see today. The point is, these types of events have been with us even before Jesus walked on the earth. They are not new, so why do we focus so heavily on them as the evidence that Jesus is rising from the throne to ready Himself for the journey to earth? Also, many Christians have suffered terribly for preaching the Gospel in the past, including many of his disciples that heard his words that day and were killed for what they believed in.

Down through the ages, many troubled *ministers* have declared that they are the Christ, with David Koresh being perhaps the latest example. So we need to ask ourselves this question: if we are pontificating the impeding return of our King, just what is it that is happening at this moment in time that points to this impending return of Jesus?

Jesus clearly has told us when the end will come. He said it is when the Gospel is preached in all the world. In other words, the end will arrive after we, his disciples, have completed the task that He assigned us just before he ascended to the right hand of God Almighty. With the advent of travel and technology, particularly the Internet, that goal has become so close. However, this book will concentrate on the often-overlooked clue that Jesus offered on that day.

And because iniquity shall abound, the love of many shall wax cold. If we put it another way because of sin and lawlessness, love will no longer abound. So who are these *many*?

The Greek translation reveals them as "the great body of people." Small words often lead to the greatest revelation. Jesus said it is *the* great body of people not *a* great body of people. The great body of people who allow their love to become cold and not enduring to the end because their focus is on sin and lawlessness is none other than us the church of Jesus Christ.

Doesn't this sound like where we are today? The discord and hate that is so palpable today either political or otherwise has leaked into the church of Jesus Christ. It has built up a wall that holds at bay the sick and the lost whom Jesus both came to seek and to save and later commissioned us to do the same. It has permeated us so deeply that many of us have decided on our own that there are some lost folk who do not deserve to hear the Gospel of Jesus Christ preached to them.

They are deemed unworthy because of the observation of this sin and lawlessness. The church has become so waxed cold and repulsed by the iniquity in the world today that it is no longer seeking to engage and losing its focus. When it does this, then Satan is the winner.

So how do we get back on track? How do we possess the same love and urgency that Jesus had for the lost? The answer is we need to go back 2,000 years ago and rediscover the simplicity of the Gospel of Jesus Christ from the words of Jesus Himself. We need to understand just what the Gospel is and then how do we effectively preach it. This will lead to a *weeding out* of our beliefs and to see clearly what our mission is in these last days before His return.

Since 2011, I can truly say that I have reminisced about at least one of the events that happened to me almost every day thereafter. They say when life gives you lemons, you make lemonade. I believe we would fare much better if when life provides the lemons give them to God for He owns the ultimate lemonade stand. All throughout the Bible and down through the ages, He has brought triumph out of defeat. He continues to confound the wise by using the simple to show simply that He *is* God.

Everyone has heard the phrase "Christmas in July," but in 2011, God allowed me to experience Christmas in June in the small town of Franklin, Tennessee. It didn't come with a plate of cookies, eggnog, or even mistletoe. It was given to me with a tall glass of God's lemonade!

Chapter 2

Mother

My mother, by all accounts, would qualify as our family matriarch. She was the one who all of us looked up to and in her later years would come to depend on. She never lost her vim and vigor or the ability to speak her mind. She was a life-long nurse and enjoyed helping people. Remarkably she was a widow on four separate occasions: having four children to her first two husbands and essentially caring for less fortunate people throughout her life.

I used to tell people that I was an only child but have one brother and two sisters of my own. (I actually have another three half sisters from my father's side, but the explanation behind this would take another book to resolve.) Yet all of us to this day don't think of ourselves as *half*. This is in no small measure due to our mother.

By 2011, my mother had reached her ninety-first year. She was residing in a nursing home in our hometown. She had moved there a few years earlier after contracting a form of Parkinson's disease that kept her from having the ability to safely walk and in particular to turn around. She never had exhibited the classic symptoms so often associated with this disease, such as trembling hands or head. That would rapidly change.

On Christmas Day 2010, my wife and I visited Mother to wish her well and give her a few presents that we had bought for her. She was seated in a wheelchair in the day room of the home. When I kissed her, I noticed that her mouth was quivering and she was having difficulty opening her mouth to speak. I must admit that I wasn't overly concerned at the time because this had happened to her before and had quickly subsided. Little did we know that this was the beginning of a perfect storm.

Less than two weeks later, my sister Cheryl, a registered nurse who was Mother's medical power of attorney, was notified that she was coughing and needed some lab work. It showed a severe respiratory infection that was also worsening her Parkinson's symptoms. Sadly she would never be able to speak again.

Things continued to deteriorate with Mother over the next two months. She started to spike fevers, and there was mounting concern that she should be admitted to the hospital at the end of February. This was no easy decision for my sister to make.

Cheryl, to her credit, was steadfast in the desire to adhere to both Mother's end of life will and subsequent conversations throughout her later years even though at times my sister's wishes may not have lined up with Mother's. Talk can be cheap, but we all know that when the rubber meets the road, so to speak, things and desires can change. Make no mistake—at this time, we were *burning rubber*.

With communication with her being reduced to eye contact, head nods, and hand squeezes, she agreed to be admitted to the hospital with a simple nod of her head.

During her two-week stay in the hospital, there were several attempts to find out just what the secret was to unlocking her jaw. It was getting so hard to see her almost hourly being poked, prodded, or radiated all the while being fed intravenously throughout her stay. Time was running out mostly due to the living will that my mother had signed and had previously been adamant to its adherence. There was to be no *heroics* in prolonging her life. The fact that she was a nurse and still mentally alert meant that she knew exactly what the choices were.

It was coming down to one solution, and it was one that with many strong squeezes of my sister's hand affirmed. Mother would not consent to the insertion of a feeding tube for her life to continue. Without it, we all were keenly aware that it would mean that her time was rapidly coming to an end.

On March 13, 2011, Mother was discharged from the hospital to go home to the nursing home for her final days. She was enrolled into hospice and directions were made to make her as comfortable as possible. I remember distinctly asking her for a favor on my last visit. I wanted her to promise me when she saw my dad to give him a big laugh by telling him that the atheist son who refused to believe in all things God-related was now a minister of the Gospel, even though I somehow believed he already knew. Her response was a turn of the head, a meeting of the eyes, and the makings of a smile through her clenched jaw.

Three days later, very early in the morning of March 18, with all her children present, she was led home to the place that Jesus promised to prepare for her. Even though her death was sad, it was also uplifting. You see, there was not one ounce of doubt as to where her destination was going to be. My brother Ted had seen to that after meeting Jesus made it his mission to preach the Gospel to all of us and led us all to the throne of grace many years before.

In the weeks before her death, God came knocking in my spirit. You see, when I put myself in a position of praise and worship, He tends to drop little phrases or desires into my heart. This time, it was a revelation that someone needed to represent our family at Mother's funeral to let everyone understand the truly remarkable life of caring that she led. It wasn't too long until I realized that it was going to me.

There was a precedent for this. Not only was I a minister at the time of my mother's death, but I also had given the eulogy at my father's funeral almost thirty-five years ago; however, this time was going to be much harder for a number of reasons.

On August 17, 1976, two weeks before departing from college for my freshman year, my father died at the age of seventy-seven. I was eighteen at the time. Yes, my father was fifty-eight years of age when I was born. The age difference and the cultural changes in the sixties and seventies made it difficult for us to relate to each other at times. My mother, being younger, often served as a buffer between us. Add the fact that he had a travel phobia that wouldn't allow him to leave our home beyond a certain radius, and it was Mother that took me to trips to the beach as well as bus trips to baseball games. I often thought it ironic that the one thing that truly bonded my father and I was baseball, but it was Mother that ended up taking me to major league games and having a catch with me in the backyard.

In the many years since his death, I have come to appreciate him much more than when I was a rebellious teenager who had embraced things like rock 'n' roll, atheism, and the long *dry* hair look! The good thing is in the years since I have matured and become a father and grandfather myself. With that appreciation and maturity, I have come to understand him much more. The exciting part is my embrace of Jesus will enable me to have those long father-son talks that we never got the chance to have in the eighteen short years we had together.

The simple fact that I had so many more years and experiences with Mother and the unconditional love she had shown me throughout my life would make it nearly impossible in my mind to eulogize her.

I can only remember one argument we ever had, and I am embarrassed to say it was on the first Thanksgiving after my father's passing. But I know my God too. If He dropped this desire in my heart, He will make a way for me to do this.

Upon praying and the guidance of the Holy Spirit, Mother's eulogy was finished in less than thirty minutes. After consulting my siblings, it was a go.

The day of her funeral arrived, and I was amazed to see the revelation of just how many people she had touched. Sure, there was family, but there were also patients that she had touched along the way during her years as a nurse.

When the ushers wheeled her simple wooded casket up the aisle of the church, I vividly remember looking at my wife as she reached out to grab my right hand. She immediately remarked how cold my hand was. I remember smiling and thinking how God has a way of pricking your spirit at just the right moment to let you know He is there for you. You see, at that moment, I flashed back to sitting with Mother in a funeral home those many years ago when she reached out to grab that same hand before my eulogy to my father and she too remarked about how cold it was. It was the very first time that I discovered the sign of nervousness. I knew at that moment everything would be all right.

Mother had gone home to be with Jesus, and we were commemorating that fact even through our sorrow and testifying to the kind of life she led. I was so grateful to both the Lord and my family that there was something I could do to help launch this celebration of the life she had here on earth as well as the one she had just embarked upon days earlier in her new eternal home. If funerals are indeed for the ones left behind, we were going to be just fine.

Chapter 3

You're Young

A week before Mother's death, I received a phone call while visiting her in the hospital from my family doctor that would ultimately change my life. I recently had my yearly physical and that included a regular set of lab work. His phone call to me was to inform me that my PSA (prostate-specific antigen) had risen again, and he wanted to refer me to a urologist for a consultation.

A rising PSA level is often a good indicator that prostate cancer could be present. Unfortunately, at that time, it was clearly a matter of when and not if Mother would pass. I used this as an excuse to put off the consultation until April.

The consultation, I guess, was a normal one under the circumstances. We talked about how the elevated PSA was steadily increasing over the past few years as well as the fact that my father had been diagnosed with prostate cancer late in his life and would be a contributing factor in his death at age seventy-seven.

In the interest of full disclosure, I am an accountant by trade, and I bring this up simply because I usually incorporate this mentality in most of the decisions that I make. For instance, when the urologist mentioned that we could do a biopsy now or simply wait six months and retake the lab test, I started to do my thing.

My father died when he was seventy-seven. I was eighteen at the time. I can remember vividly even to this day the memory of my sisters taking me to see the movie the *Jungle Book* when I was nine years old. It was a way of keeping me occupied while my mom and dad could discuss his diagnosis of prostate cancer and the prognosis of his future. The cancer was advanced, and at that time, there were few choices and methods to combat it. He was given about ten years.

Being a stubborn man, he took way too long to get to the doctor's office for initial treatment; and sure enough, six weeks after my high school graduation and two weeks before I entered college, he was gone. It was ten years since the diagnosis. As I sat in the doctor's office at my appointment, I did the math and came up with the realization since prostate cancer is a slowly progressing disease that he probably had it at about my current age of fifty-three. This accounting exercise made the decision easier—a biopsy it was. We would know the results in a week.

I arrived at the follow-up appointment with my wife the next week to get the results. I must admit I wasn't too apprehensive due to the fact that the doctor had commented during the biopsy that the prostate didn't appear to be too enlarged. That small fragment of hope that I reminisced about during that week quickly evaporated. In a few minutes, we sat devastated. The results showed that not only did I have prostate cancer, but it was also moderately advanced and had the possibility of leaving the prostate if not treated soon. The doctor then explained the various options that were available for the treatment of this cancer. I must admit I don't even remember most anything he said other than he would recommend an appointment with his partner who was well versed in robotic surgery to discuss specific surgical options that were available.

I have worked for one of the most renowned plastic surgeons in our area for more than eleven years. In the course of my work, I have met and became familiar with a local oncologist during that time. I immediately made an appointment to see him that very day. He again would give me the various courses of action that could be taken for treatment. After all was said and done, there was only one realistic option for me, and that was surgery.

In guiding me to this decision, the oncologist said something that would stay with me during this entire time. He told me that the decision was an easy one for him to recommend simply because *you're young*.

The next week, I had my presurgical appointment with the surgical urologist. Upon thoroughly explaining the robotic surgery, he threw me a curve. He said he would highly recommend that I have the surgery not here but at John's Hopkins Medical Center in Baltimore, Maryland. It would be a three-day stay barring complications. The reason that he gave was that I would have a better long-term outcome there because *you're young*. I remember thinking that I may be young, but the logistics would make it hard on my wife and family to travel there. Did I have any other options? I didn't know but I knew who would—my sister Cheryl.

Everyone in the family knows that, for medical advice, you call my sister. She worked in nursing administration at UPMC Pinnacle hospital in Harrisburg, Pennsylvania, which was a mere eighteen miles from my home. Surely she would know what to do and whom to call.

THE CHRISTMAS TREE EFFECT

Within an hour after placing the call to her, my cell phone rang. It was Dr. Scott Owens, a urologist based in Camp Hill, Pennsylvania. He instructed me to come in to see him later that afternoon. It was May 20. The fact that it was a Friday afternoon impressed me.

Upon meeting Dr. Owens, my wife and I recognized there was a peace that came over us. This was important because I have always preached that God's answers come wrapped in peace and Dr. Owens was caring and there was a definite air of confidence about him. That peacefulness we felt in his office made the decision easy. There was only one thing left to do and that was to schedule the surgery.

The first confirmation of how good a physician Dr. Owens was could be found in the fullness of his surgical schedule. That fact, along with his scheduled vacation, put the date of surgery at July 28. I felt the disappointment knowing that this insidious disease would be left slowly growing inside of me for another two months, but I was reassured that it would make little difference. I admit I am not a very patient man (more on that later) and I remember thinking maybe it doesn't matter to you, but it means a great deal to me. The thought I had to wait over two months to get this agent of death out of me was almost too much for me to bear. Yes, I admit I was flat scared! That fear led to many sleepless nights that I spent going upstairs and praying to God and crying in the dark. I just wanted this out of me now! Little did I know then nor did I bother to ask Him, but this delay was all part of God's plan.

The day finally arrived for the first major surgery of my life. Even though Dr. Owens had thoroughly explained the procedure and its aftermath to me, I was understandably apprehensive. It didn't help that in the weeks before my surgery, I read in our local newspaper that the hospital where the surgery was scheduled had just put into operation a brand-new upgraded robotic surgical device. You might think that would be a good thing, and it actually was; but I remember when I read the article thinking if Dr. Owens was going to be as familiar with this robot as he had been with the past one. Of course, my first question to him when he met me at the hospital was whether he had *test driven* it yet. He smiled that easygoing smile of his and assured me that all was well. Now that I think of it, I don't remember whether or not he actually answered my question to my satisfaction.

Teresa had been with me all the way on this journey, and she was truly remarkable. We cried together, we laughed together, we worried together, and most importantly, we prayed together leading up to and including this day.

While sitting in the prep area holding hands, *that* woman appeared and made her promised entrance. Here she was again, my sister Cheryl. As promised, she was here to provide me with moral support, but more importantly, she was here for Teresa. She would spend the length of the surgery until recovery with Teresa. In a way it would be more difficult for Teresa than me. I got to *sleep* through this long procedure where she would have to endure the waiting for hours until the good news finally came. The time had now arrived.

Upon being wheeled into the operating room, the first thing I noticed was how cold it was. That was remedied quickly by a nurse providing me with a heated blanket. Dr. Owens made his introductions, including the robot. His final intro was the anesthesiologist. I honestly do not remember his name or face. He explained that he was going to administer the anesthesia; and the very next thing I knew I was waking up in the recovery room.

THE CHRISTMAS TREE EFFECT

Not long after Dr. Owens informed me that the operation was a success and that he had informed Teresa of that fact, I still was in no condition to see just exactly what the effects of the surgery were.

That would come the next morning when I was allowed to walk again. I went into the bathroom and opened my robe. You can be told, even with the highest degree of specificity, something but nothing prepares you with actually seeing it. There the mirror revealed just what needed to take place in order to eradicate this disease from my body. There were several entrance wounds that were filled with what looked to me like black silly putty. There was also sort of a stab wound from which a drain emanated.

Before surgery, I told Dr. Owens that I would like to go home the day after the surgery. He was hesitant but promised to allow me to do so if I felt up to it. The image staring back at me at that moment made me know that I wasn't feeling up to it. I wanted to stay another day.

The operation was on Thursday morning, and I was discharged on Saturday allowing me to preach to my small but mighty congregation the next day. The fact that I am writing this book seven years later proves the success of the procedure, but there was one hiccup.

After following Dr. Owens every six months for the first three years, he shocked me in September 2014. The results of my most recent PSA test had shown an uptick. It was no longer *undetectable*. Beating this cancer was going to be even tougher than I thought.

The appointment was made with the radiation oncologist at the Cancer Center in my town. The long-ride home was quiet. I usually call my wife on my cell phone after each appointment to give her the good news. This time, this news could not be given with a simple phone call because the appointment was longer than I had planned.

There was no reason to return to work, so I immediately headed home. There was a very different conversation that awaited me there.

I can remember when my wife arrived that she was surprised to see me there. That surprise didn't even come close to measuring up to the news that I broke that late early fall day.

She asked me the same question that I had just about an hour ago in Dr. Owens' office: "What now?" I wish that I had a firm grasp of the situation that I could explain it to her, but I was just as shell-shocked now as she was. The feeling that I had was that same feeling I felt three years ago with my original diagnosis. All I knew for sure was there was going to be radiation involved. At the first mention of radiation, I wondered if this was going to cause my hair to fall out. That was a strange thought indeed since I didn't have much hair to begin with. It is truly amazing how you can feel so well only to have that same feeling morph into a feeling of utter despair the very next moment. Even though I thought I was done with this cancer, it was now obvious that it was not quite done with me.

I remember having a fleeting thought of rolling the dice and opting not to have this treatment because prostate cancer is a notorious slow but deadly mover. Again I was told that there was no really good option other than radiation by my oncologist because as he reminded me, "You're young."

Once again, God was there every step of the way.

The treatments began in late September and lasted until early November. I remember with each treatment and with each side effect of the radiation that my goal was to finish before Thanksgiving, so that I could fully participate in our family's traditional get together and feast.

In all, there were thirty-seven treatments, five days each week for seven and a half weeks. These treatments culminated in a PSA test in early December.

Upon delivering the results, my oncologist simply said, "Merry Christmas. The results were undetectable."

I truly am grateful for this and every undetectable test that I have taken since.

As I approach the seventh year since the surgery and the fourth year since radiation therapy, I have graduated to a yearly follow-up examination and PSA. I am still cancer-free and intend to be that way until I follow my mother and father to the place that my Jesus has prepared for me. After all, I am still young!

Chapter 4

Grace Amazing: New Life in the Face of Death

As I alluded before, the year 2011 was a roller coaster of year that included new life in the face of death and uncertainty. In nature, it seems that new life always surfaces in the face of death. Agriculture experts say that new tree seedlings always emerge after a forest fire. The heat from the fire helps to crack open the pine cones that release thousands of new seeds that in turn produce new seedlings, that will produce the trees that will eventually replace those lost in the original fire. In fact, Jesus alludes to this principle spiritually when he tells the disciples in John 12:24 (KJV), "Verily, verily I say unto you, except a corn of wheat fall into the ground and die, it abideth alone: but if it die, it bringeth forth much fruit."

All during my mother's struggle and ultimate death, as well as the diagnosis of cancer, there was another event that was rapidly heading toward its conclusion that year.

My daughter Shannon was pregnant with her first child and about to present us with our first grandchild. She and her husband had opted to have the sex of the child revealed to them, and upon hearing that they were having a girl, the irony struck me. My mother had six grandchildren before Shannon was born, and all six were boys. She had voiced many times that she had given up the idea of a granddaughter. That fact led to a sublime encounter immediately after Shannon arrived.

My oldest sister, Beverly, was having surgery and was hospitalized on the day of my daughter's birth. (God is always on time.) Labor, as it often does, ended in its good old time. As I have always told her, Shannon was being stubborn and delaying her arrival. She would eventually arrive after hospital visiting hours were over. That deterrent failed to stop Mother who quietly remained in Beverly's room to await the birth of her seventh grandson, or so she believed.

I will never forget the moment when I presented her with her first granddaughter. I was holding Shannon in my arms and, with a smile on my face, told her that she had her long-awaited granddaughter. Her reaction was priceless, to say the least. Citing my proclivity to be a prankster, she did not hesitate to tell me that she was not going to believe my words. She then proceeded to lift the blanket, and once making sure that Shannon's anatomy did indeed confirm my words, she left out a little shriek and her eyes filled with tears. Sadly, although Mother knew Shannon was pregnant late in 2010, she would not live to see her first great-granddaughter.

I vividly remember when I held my granddaughter for the first time that fateful encounter on the night she was born between Mother and Shannon and realized how proud she would be at that moment. My thought quickly raced to the name that her parents had bestowed on her. Here in this moment, born after Mother's death and my diagnosis but before the surgery that was set to eradicate this cancer from me, I was holding a precious little girl called Grace… Amazing!

Chapter 5

Why Am I Here?

As I mentioned earlier, the events of the first half of the year were all intertwined. Aside from my mother's death and the diagnosis of cancer there was yet another event that was demanding my attention at the time. Timing wise it sat in between the death of my mother, the diagnosis of cancer and the surgery itself, along with the birth of Grace. It was a delightful gesture at first but was increasingly becoming a problem under the present circumstances. Remarkably, through all of the life-changing events that I experienced that year, this event would involve the one encounter that would affect my life and ministry more than any other and is the subject of this book.

At that time, I was pastoring a small church in Carlisle, Pennsylvania, that my wife and I had started a couple of years earlier. Now anyone who has spent a considerable amount of time with me or had attended one of our church services would know that Michael W. Smith was extremely important to me even though we had never met. Michael is perhaps the most decorated and honored contemporary Christian artist of this generation. Countless times his music and I would argue his ministry was exactly what I needed even in the darkest times.

I have always remembered the many summer days floating in a tiny blow-up pool in my backyard behind a rickety homemade fence that I installed. To get the full effect of this scene, you have to believe that I am in no way or shape a carpenter. I knew instinctively that I would someday tear it down, so I never bothered to cement the posts in the ground. Also, the backyard was not level by any stretch of the imagination, but I did my best to level it off before inflating the pool. It ended up having a little tilt to it, but I deemed it *good enough*.

So each sunny day, my wife and I would mount our *floaties* and spend the afternoon in the pool bumping into each other with the music of Michael W. Smith playing in the background. The album of choice was *The First Decade* (1983–1993). The song we loved the most was the first one on the album, "Do You Dream of Me." This song continues to mean so much to us even after all this time.

How much? It was on my Christmas list this year because my original copy was skipping. It is one we have floated to, the one we have danced to and lyrics of which my wife included in her last of the over *750* letters that she wrote to me on the eve of my freedom after over two years of incarceration. I had always made it a ritual to search his website for news and new music.

One day, I noticed that there was going to be something new being offered to his "friends online"—Michael was putting together what was called a Tennessee Weekend to be held June 3–5, 2011. It would be an opportunity to visit Michael in his hometown Franklin, Tennessee, for three days. In fact, on Saturday night June 3, there was scheduled to be a barbeque to be held at his farm.

I thought this would be an amazing experience and no doubt expressed this to the congregation at some point.

Shortly after my mother's death and before being diagnosed with prostate cancer, my wife asked to come to the podium one Sunday and asked to speak. My wife is very shy about public speaking, so I thought this was odd and probably pretty important.

When she announced that the congregation had decided that they wanted to send me to the Tennessee weekend, I was speechless. As excited as I was that Sunday, the rug was pulled out from under me later upon hearing the cancer diagnosis. The eradication from my body of this disease was the most important thing in my life at that point. Sadly, I thought I had no choice but to cancel this once-in-a-lifetime opportunity.

On the following Monday morning upon hearing my diagnosis, I called the travel agent who was handling this event and explained that under the circumstances, I felt that I would need to cancel. The representative regretfully informed me that since the representative of our congregation had not secured travel insurance, a refund was not possible.

Between the pity party that I was throwing for myself and the fact that our small church would suffer the loss of the money that it had graciously spent, I started to reconsider.

The fact that the Tennessee Weekend was less than two weeks away and my surgery wasn't until the end of July made the decision somewhat easier. I was going to go after all. I became convinced that this convergence of events the first half of the year were no accident. I convinced myself that God was truly working in this mess somewhere and I became determined to find out what He was up to. As I began walking up the jet way after landing in Nashville, I remember vividly asking God, "Okay, Why am I here?" It was certainly not the last time I would ask that question during weekend especially when more lemons began to appear!

By the time the church had signed me up for the Tennessee Weekend, the allotted rooms at the host hotel were booked. This meant that I had to make reservations at one of the satellite hotels that remained. Registration, however, still took place at the host hotel. My taxi arrived at the host hotel later than I had hoped. I noticed that I was obviously one of the last to register. Therefore, there were no more shuttles available to my hotel. God, why was I here again?

As I began to panic, a gentleman with a Michael W. Smith & Friends Tennessee Weekend T-shirt appeared and asked me if everything was all right. I explained my dilemma, and much to my surprise, he offered to drive me to my hotel in his personal car. I would find out later in the evening that he was an assistant to Michael W. Smith. I gratefully accepted his offer.

Once I had safely checked into my hotel, I quickly unpacked and got ready to catch the shuttle bus to a facility called Rocketown in downtown Nashville, Tennessee.

Rocketown was founded by Mr. Smith in 1994 and is described as a place that was established to "to give teens a positive alternative to the many pressures that they face." It includes an entertainment space and an indoor skate park.

Dinner was the first event of the weekend, followed by a group photo and then a concert by the host himself. I was anxious to get the weekend started when I boarded the shuttle bus at my hotel.

After a brief amount of time to allow everyone onto the bus, off we went! We had traveled a grand total of about one hundred yards when the bus lurched forward and stalled. There was nothing to be alarmed at as it was restarted and began to move forward.

THE CHRISTMAS TREE EFFECT

Again, as quickly as before, the bus stalled. This time, there would be no restart. After a few minutes, a person appeared at the front of the bus to announce that we would have to get off and wait for another bus to be dispatched and pick us up.

Isn't it funny at times when you are full of anticipation things that would normally be obvious to you actually become oblivious?

Upon leaving the bus, it took me only a few moments to become aware of the extreme heat. It was then that I remembered that the forecast for the entire weekend was sunny and hot with temperatures in the nineties. There was also the shrill sound of cicadas all around me.

In Pennsylvania, this sound is only reserved for late July or early August.

Sweating and annoyed, I perceived the answer to the question of why I was here was becoming obvious, or so I thought.

I am not by any stretch of the imagination a patient man. In fact, impatience and inconvenience have caused strife in my life on a number of occasions.

Surely this entire weekend was meant to test my patience, and I decided while sweating in that driveway that I was going to pass this test.

The second bus arrived to pick us up about a half hour later. I was happy to see it and felt the air-conditioning as I boarded.

We arrived at Rocketown around six thirty, which was thirty minutes late for the start of dinner. I had to fight back the thought of the inconvenience that this was causing me. After all, isn't this why I was here, to work out my impatience?

Word had arrived to Michael's group that there was a bus that had broken down and they delayed the festivities until we arrived.

It was soon after I was seated that Michael appeared in the front of the room. At the end of his welcome, he made the statement that it had come to his attention of the unfortunate circumstances of a bus breaking down on its way to Rocketown. He declared that for the rest of the weekend, those persons on that bus would have reserved seating at the front of all the remaining events starting with the concert that night! My first *A* on my patience test was here. The test was far from over.

After dinner, we were all herded to the parking lot for a group photo. It required everyone to be close together within a circle.

There was a cameraman hoisted high above the area with a lift. By my estimation, there were at least a couple hundred people in attendance. Did I mention it was hot? Naturally it took some time to get this amount of humans in the right position in the camera shot.

Upon getting all of us into position, the cameraman asked us if we thought there was something missing. "Do you think Michael should be in the picture?" the cameraman asked.

Of course, the answer was a resounding yes!

After a minute or two, the crowd parted, and there he was face-to-face with me, Michael W. Smith. I didn't say a word but extended my hand, and he shook it. We were then instructed to look upward and wave, and then the photo was taken.

Now I will tell you that I have indeed washed that hand many times over the past seven years, but I still have and wear the bright yellow shirt to this day!

Another *A* on the test I thought as we headed back inside to tour Rocketown and then find my reserved seat for the concert to come.

After I returned to my hotel room that night, the words of a dear friend of mine rang in my head. He would tell me that, in moments like these, I needed to have some note paper available and be prepared to record what God might be up to. I began my weekend *diary* before going to bed. Little did I know that when the weekend was over, there would be a revelation on those pages—a revelation from the Holy Spirit that would literally change both my life and ministry to this very day. Unbeknownst to me, there was just one more test to pass.

This next and most important test of patience would arrive the next day. The final night of the Tennessee Weekend was on Saturday. It would entail a trip to Deer Valley Farm in Franklin, Tennessee. This was not just your average farm. It belonged to our host, Michael W. Smith. He was hosting a barbecue and afterward a special acoustical concert with a few of his singer/songwriter friends.

It would start at four o'clock and was on the hottest day of the weekend. The temperature was flirting with triple digits, and the farm was about a mile off the main road. Several water stations were set up along the pathway that led to the barbeque. Everyone was encouraged to take as much water as we needed. The walk was uneventful and even pleasant as the trail to the farm winded through a long path lined with trees, but I must admit the heat and humidity were taking their toll primarily on my shirt.

But there in the distance was the end of the trail and at the end an immaculate barn. Just beyond this barn was a tethered multicolored hot-air balloon (my memory of which is quite specific due to my apprehension of heights). To the left was one of the largest tents I had ever seen right in the middle of a pasture. This was the venue of the Tennessee barbeque.

After arriving at the venue, I remember telling myself to take a seat and be perfectly still. Maybe I would stop sweating if I could just keep still. Much to my amazement it worked!

The food was great, and the entertainment even better. Not even another mile trek to the buses that awaited our trip home to the hotels could dampen my spirit—shirt, yes; but spirit, no!

As I entered the bus, my cell phone rang, and it was my wife. I remember telling her that it was hot and how I perceived my patience test was going this evening. She was very well-aware (and still is I perceive) of my need for more patience, so much so that I was beginning to believe that she was in on this with God, especially with her approval of how things were transpiring and developing. I remained on the phone with her all during my trip to the hotel.

When the bus pulled into the driveway, I told her I loved her and went to my room. It was time for this day's entry into my diary and then to bed; however, God had another splendid idea.

When I was finished with my entry, I remember sitting back in my chair at the hotel desk with a smile. There was only a half day left in this trip, and I was somewhat pleased that God had begun a good work in me. Turning to James 1:4, I read, "But let patience have her perfect work, that ye may be perfect and entire, wanting nothing." It was then that I thought, *If I am to want nothing, then what does God want of me?* The answer was almost instantaneous.

Chapter 6

Christmas in June

Taking my pen in my hand, I turned to a blank sheet of paper and began to draw. This is no small development because I have already confessed to be an accountant, and that profession and artistic expression normally do not travel on parallel lines.

When I was finished, I saw that it was a tree, specifically it was a pine tree, albeit one in need of some horticultural help but nevertheless a pine tree. You could even argue that it was a Christmas tree. How odd it was for me to draw a Christmas tree in June on one of the hottest, most humid days I had ever known!

My mind or my spirit, I am still not sure which, suddenly remembered the many times my dear wife and I had set out on the Saturday morning after Thanksgiving for the task of finding a Christmas tree for our house. It is a meticulous exercise, to say the least. I suspect and, in fact, have observed over the years that our experience was not unique.

On the contrary, I truly believe that no one sets out to find the perfect Charlie Brown tree. For us, there is always walking through the rows of precut trees and finding one that might be a candidate, pulling it out, and twirling it while my wife inspects it for possible perfection. This is usually multiplied several times until the closest thing to perceived perfection is found, purchased, shaken, twined, and then placed in our car for the journey to its new home.

After a few cuts and trimming, it is then placed in our living room and placed in the perfect spot. Throughout the years, we always would then delay decorating the tree until Sunday night with our entire blended family present. It is a ritual that for the most part has survived, even though there is just the two of us remaining.

As I sat staring at this primitive work of art on my paper in front of me, I started to get a real sense that there was something that God was trying to get me to understand. I began drawing ornaments and lights on this tree to the point that the tree was getting harder and harder to see clearly. The thought occurred to me that after all the meticulous (and sometimes exhausting) hunt for the perfect tree, it was an odd exercise to then go about *covering it up* with all our decorations, even though this is the tradition.

From the time the tree is decorated to the time it is torn down, no one really sees the simple beauty of this *perfect* tree that was so carefully chosen and brought home that lies beneath the *clutter* of decorations.

It was during this thought the Holy Spirit burst into my spirit with a revelation that is still as exciting today as it was at that very moment. You see, this act of concealment of our tree is the same way Christians *decorate* and conceal the Gospel of Jesus Christ.

Many years ago, there were games of *skill* called pinball machines that I used to play. When shaken too much or too hard, they would stop working and display the word *tilt*. This is exactly how my brain was feeling. It had *tilted*, and I had just enough sense left to begin to pray for the proof of this revelation. I prayed specifically asking that I need proof, and for the next several hours, the Spirit of the living God began to provide it.

It began with a question that was posed inside my spirit: just what is the Gospel of Jesus Christ? I knew Paul's letter to the Romans says, "For I am not ashamed of the gospel of Christ, for it is the power of God to salvation for everyone who believes" (Romans 1:16, NKJV).

This explanation seemed more like what it does or what it represents than what is actually is. What exactly is it, and why is God equating it to a Christmas tree? I pondered.

The tree that we always attempt to pick out each year is simple yet majestic. It is strong enough to support all our ornaments. It is always there beneath the decorations. It is always there underneath, providing the strength and substance to make the presentation of the decorations more beautiful. It is the one thing that actually makes the beauty of the decorations work not vice versa.

Since this is the Gospel *of* Christ, I needed to see what Jesus said about it, and what better place to start than when he commissioned the disciples and us to preach it. I wanted to see exactly what he told them each time he was admonishing them to preach the Gospel and specifically how Matthew, Mark, Luke, and John recorded it.

Matthew recorded in the twenty-eighth chapter,

> Go therefore and make disciples of all the nations, baptizing them in the name of the Father and of the Son and of the Holy Spirit, teaching them to observe all things that I have commanded you; and lo, I am with you always, *even* to the end of the age. Amen. (Matthew 28:19–20, NKJV)

It seems that Matthew believed the importance of Jesus's last encounter was simply to go and teach, make disciples, and baptize. But specifically, what are we to preach and teach? Maybe Mark will shed more light on it.

This same final encounter between Jesus and His disciples is found in the sixteenth chapter of Mark. He records Jesus as saying, "And He said to them, 'Go into all the world and preach the gospel to every creature. He who believes and is baptized will be saved; but he who does not believe will be condemned'" (Mark 16:15–16, NKJV).

So in other words, Matthew records that Jesus tells us to preach, and now Mark says that Jesus commands us to preach the Gospel. But the question remains: just what is the Gospel? Maybe the answer is in what Luke recorded, I thought.

Luke records this same great commission a little differently with more details and finally some clarities as to what Jesus considers to actually be the Gospel.

There are times in my walk that I have received a revelation from God that was exciting, but this time, as I sat at the hotel desk, my spirit exploded inside me when I saw the words recorded in the twenty-fourth chapter of Luke. Would it shock you to know that the Gospel really consisted of five words? Five words!

Jesus is recorded in Luke 24:46–47 (NKJV) as saying, "Then He said to them, 'Thus it is written; and thus it is necessary for the Christ to suffer and to rise from the dead the third day, and that *repentance and remission of sins* should be preached in His name to all nations, beginning in Jerusalem.'"

In that moment, staring back at me were the words that formed the simple yet majestic strength of the Gospel of Christ. Repentance and remission of sins form that perfect *Christmas tree* that we are always searching for. These five words form the strong trunk that is able to sprout strong symmetrical branches that are prepared to help support and maintain spiritual life. These words have been hidden under *ornaments* that have been hung on them that *result from* the acceptance of the Gospel, such as gaining heaven as our home or, as the Lord Jesus Himself said in Luke 4:18–19, healing our broken hearts, being set free from oppression, and regaining our ability to see again.

But perhaps the one thing that has been hung on the tree of the Gospel that surely doesn't belong is something that ironically has been covered by the blood of Jesus—sin itself. Either way, these *ornaments* obscure the simple message of forgiveness that God wants us to convey to a dying world.

These five simple words of repentance and remission of sins are so powerful that once they are preached and enter into a sinner's heart, they transform it to one that is alive and quicken our spirit with the joining of His.

Chapter 7

What Has Sin Got to Do with It?

As I sat back in my chair on that sultry early June night in my hotel, the enormity of this revelation began to hit me in a very simple way. The question that was in my mind at that moment was that if *repentance and remission of sins* were truly the Gospel of Jesus Christ that I was commissioned to preach, then just how do I preach it? Better yet, as a pastor, how do I teach others to preach it? I thought that it would take only one Sunday sermon. The truth is I have preached this message for the past seven years and haven't even scratched the surface. But the most important revelation that I received that night and have continued to be made crystal clear to me by the Spirit of God is not what I should preach but what I should *not* preach.

Sadly, on any given Sunday in churches all over this nation and others the dominant topic that is preached is sin. It is front and center in the majority of the sermons delivered from their pulpits. It is so prevalent that you would think that Jesus defined the Gospel as only *repentance and sin* leaving out the *remission* part of it. You see, Jesus came to remit sin through the shedding of His blood not to shine a bright light on it. He was hung on a tree, so we would never need to hang sin on our *Christmas tree*.

I find it astonishing that perhaps the most memorized and recited verse in the entire Bible is John 3:16 (KJV): "For God so loved the world, that he gave his only begotten Son, that whosoever believeth in him should not perish, but have everlasting life."

But the one that immediately comes after it is virtually ignored by comparison. John 3:17 (KJV) says, "For God sent not his Son into the world to condemn the world; but that the world through him might be saved."

I would argue that verse 17 may be even more the more impactful verse. Let me explain: without John 3:17, God could not even send Jesus in the first place. It explains exactly how God so loved the world that he gave His only Son. He could *not* send Him to condemn the world if the mission was to save it. Nevertheless, the problem immediately at hand for me that night in June of 2011 was trying to understand just how Jesus expected me to preach this Gospel.

A thought then occurred to me.

Since I had learned so much from the first three authors who recorded the ministry of Jesus, it just made sense to see what John's take on this encounter was. Indeed, true to my suspicions, John, the apostle that Jesus loved as he was fond of saying, had the answer.

In John 20:20–23, he gives a stunning and remarkable recording of Jesus's words saying that what lies in front of us is a task that makes the Christian walk the challenge that Jesus both warned and promised it would be.

The King James version gave a more accurate account of His words.

> And when he had so said, he shewed unto them his hands and his side. Then were the disciples glad, when they saw the Lord. Then said Jesus to them again, Peace be unto you: as my Father hath sent me, even so send I you. And when he had said this, he breathed on them, and saith unto them, Receive ye the Holy Ghost: Whosoever sins ye remit, they are remitted unto them; and whosoever sins ye retain, they are retained.

As I read these verses in my hotel room on that late Saturday night, my spirit exploded! There it was in red and white: "As the Father has sent Me, I also send you." The torch has been passed to us. Jesus said He was sent to preach the Gospel to the poor, and He is telling us in John 20:23 that the most effective way to preach the Gospel isn't necessarily in the words that we say but the forgiveness that we offer.

What was true then is even more so today. People will watch what you do far more than listen to what you say. That is why the words that are attributed to Francis of Assisi ring so true to me when he said to "preach always and when necessary use words."

Forgiveness is the heart and soul of the Gospel. It is the very act of remitting sins. It was the prerequisite for the relationship that God promised to restore from the fall of Adam to the day of Pentecost. God knew that in order to make the rebirth possible, He had to go first.

The Old Testament is clear in its writings that sin was the barrier to reestablish our relationship with the Creator. Moses had to be protected from the glory of God, lest He be incinerated by it. Only the chief priest was allowed to enter the Holy of Holies in order to offer the sacrifices for the people of God. Even then he was required to wear a bell to notify the people that he had made a misstep and a rope to pull his lifeless body from the inner chamber.

Now the Bible tells us that that same glory resides in us due to God's removal of this barrier. Repentance by us would be pointless and remain fatal if sin had not been remitted. If we truly believe that Jesus was indeed the once and for all sacrifice for our sin, then the barrier is down and the only step remaining is repentance.

Preaching sin and putting a constant focus on it simply builds that wall of separation back up or puts decorations on the tree of the Gospel that has no business being there.

Do I believe that there is no longer sin in the world? Of course there is! However, I refuse to spend all of my time and energy concentrating on the very thing that the blood of Jesus was shed to cover! In fact, Paul writes in Colossians 2:13–14 that God *has* (present tense) forgiven *all* of our trespasses and went even further by, in effect, wiping out the debt we had by nailing it to the cross. It is also clear from the interaction that John recorded in his Gospel that our focus as disciples of Christ must be dispensing—for example, remitting people's sins and not pointing them out. If the Gospel by its very definition is good news, then what is good news about constantly making us painfully aware that we are just sinners?

The good news this world needs so badly today is that we *were* sinners, but we are now saved by grace—the grace of forgiveness!

The prophet Micah records in Micah 7:19 that "He (God) will turn again, He will have compassion upon us: He will subdue our iniquities; and Thou will cast all of our sins into the depth of the sea."

Unfortunately, we, at one time or another, have all donned the scuba gear of judgment that brought these drowned sins to the surface. In fact, I believe that focusing on someone's sin is a form of judgment, and we have specifically been told not to judge (Matthew 7:1; Romans 2:1).

I offer the following verses in 2 Corinthians chapter 5, which I believe both beautifully defines the Gospel of Jesus Christ as well as the ministry that Jesus gave us in the great commission.

> Therefore, if anyone is in Christ, he is a new creation; old things have passed away; behold, all things have become new. Now all things are of God, who has reconciled us to Himself through Jesus Christ, and has given us the ministry of reconciliation, that is, that God was in Christ reconciling the world to Himself, not imputing their trespasses to them, and has committed to us the word of reconciliation. Now then, we are ambassadors for Christ, as though God were pleading through us: we implore you on Christ's behalf, be reconciled to God.

With these four short verses, Paul gave a name to the Gospel of Jesus Christ—the Ministry of Reconciliation—and thus, it is that ministry that we are to preach.

Reconciliation is indeed the focal point of the Gospel as it is mentioned five times in one form or another in these verses. Reconciliation, by its very nature, must include forgiveness to be successful. In fact, reconciliation is impossible without it.

If I may paraphrase these verses, Paul was saying,

> You are a new creation if you are in Christ. All your past is gone, and what remains is all of God. He has reconciled all of us to Himself through Jesus and in return has given us a ministry, an ambassadorship, to go and preach this; that God

was personally present in Christ while reconciling the world to Himself all the while *not* holding our sins against us and has promised us the word of reconciliation which is forgiveness.

Alas, the Gospel that we are to preach has been replaced in today's Christianity by the exact opposite. It is what I call the Ministry of Separation. By that, I mean, we are encouraged to preach and teach what separates us *from* God (sin) instead of what He did to reconcile us *to* Him (forgiveness). In preaching sin, we are keeping people away from what they so desperately need today or should I say from whom they so desperately need?

Chapter 8

Preaching Like Jesus

How do I preach the Gospel of Jesus Christ? Better yet, how do I preach like Jesus? After all, He told us that He was anointed to preach the Gospel to the poor. In fact, as I have mentioned before, He declared to the disciples that He was sending them and in turn us as the Father had sent Him.

Paul admonished us in Philippians 2:5 to "let this mind be in you that was also in Christ Jesus." To do this means that we need to have a full understanding of just what was the end game that God through Jesus accomplished.

For at least the past six years, I have asked the following question when I have witnessed to others, and I have yet to receive what I believe is a correct response. Oh, I know that most of the answers that I received have been partially correct but never go to the heart of the mission that Jesus so humbly signed up for.

The correct answer requires a full understanding and belief in something that has been portrayed as unbelievable and thus unattainable. The question that I ask is simply this: why did God send Jesus?

THE CHRISTMAS TREE EFFECT

The responses vary from "to save us" to "so we can be forgiven for our sins" to "so we can go to heaven" to "so we can receive the Holy Spirit." As I said, most of these answers to my question have a certain truth in them but never quite hit the bullseye. You see, Jesus indeed came to save us and in doing so we are forgiven for our sins. By accepting His sacrifice, we do, in fact, have an opportunity to reunite in heaven; and as Jesus told us in John 14:16, He most assuredly prayed, and the Father sent us another Helper in the Holy Ghost.

The overwhelming reason that God sent Jesus can be found tucked inside the word that is mentioned five times in various forms within the definition of the Gospel of Jesus Christ in 2 Corinthians 5:17–20. That word is *reconciliation*.

By remitting our sins, or as Paul says, "not imputing our trespasses unto us," God provided the means to extend to us the possibility of reconciliation, and there is a certain benefit achieved through this reconciliation and that is a *relationship*, a *friendship*.

God sent Jesus into the world to remit our sins so that the relationship that God had with Adam and Eve before they betrayed Him in the Garden of Eden would now be available to all who repent. It is that simple and yet that profound.

Preaching like Jesus literally means "as the Father sent me, even so send I you." It means we have the ministry of reconciliation, and that God is now in us through the Holy Spirit reconciling the world to Himself. The torch has been passed by the *great commission*. So I must ask you this question: if God forgave us *all* our trespasses and did not hold these trespasses against us and Jesus successfully finished His mission as the *once and for all* sacrifice for sin, then why do we still use sin to get people to repent?

I get that the wages of sin is death. I get that sin is still here to tempt us and make us fall. I get that sin can still prevent us from receiving all that God has for us, but I also know that if I sin and truly repent, asking for forgiveness that I have a High Priest and advocate with the Father who is faithful and just to forgive me of my sins and cleanses me from all unrighteousness (1 John 1:9).

The key to this verse is that He is both faithful *and* forgives us of our sin. It means that not only will he forgive us, but he also has the right to do so. Jesus is our advocate, which means he is our attorney, if you will. He has the right to advocate on our behalf in front of God to rebut the accusations of Satan. He is better than any Perry Mason. He has never lost a case.

Therefore, I have personally made the decision that I will not dwell on something that has been defeated and placed under the blood of Jesus. In fact, I believe by pointing out and thus using people's sins to get them to repent is actually a form of judgment, and we were warned by Jesus not to judge.

I know what the next question is. It is always the next question I am asked: "Pastor, if we don't use sin to convince people that they are sinners, then how do we get them to repent?"

God actually gives us what we need to achieve this repentance. In Romans 2:4 (KJV), Paul writes, "Or despisest thou the riches of his goodness and forebearance and longsuffering; not knowing that the goodness of God leadeth thee to repentance?"

The goodness of God leads to repentance, not the judgment of God, not the fear of hell, and not the wrath of God. The goodness of God leads to repentance. Repentance—it is the last remaining item that stands in the way of a reconciliation and relationship with God.

Preaching and teaching the goodness of God and thus the message of the Gospel require us to take the time to truly get to know and become intimate with the Messenger.

For two and a half years, I had the opportunity to tune much of the world out and develop a deeper relationship with Him. I learned that He is absolute. There is no lukewarm about Him. It is black and white and no gray. Above all, He *is* love. He doesn't just have it. He doesn't just give it. He couldn't help Himself. Even when we were enemies, Ephesians tells us He came because of His great love for us. After all, He *is* love!

CHAPTER 9

Raymond—The Proof of the Pudding

Jesus said in Luke 12:48 (KJV), "For unto whomsoever much is given, of him shall be much required: and to whom men have committed much, of him they will ask the more."

I had been aware of this passage in the past, and I was sure that it would become relevant to me in a short period of time when God felt that I was ready to start walking in this amazing revelation that He had bestowed upon me. However, I must admit that I was not seeking this *requirement* as diligently as when I was initially seeking the meaning or purpose of why I was in Nashville in June of 2011.

As I wrote earlier in May of 2012, I was pastoring a small church in my hometown of Carlisle, Pennsylvania, when I received a call after a Sunday service from a dear friend telling me of her father's sudden serious illness. She and her family were members of a congregation of a church that I had helped to pastor on an interim basis, and we had remained close. She informed me that her father had been rushed to a medical center outside of Harrisburg, Pennsylvania, and asked if I could visit him and the family at the hospital.

Upon arriving, I visited Gary in the intensive care unit only to be shocked at his appearance. He was obviously very weak and was encumbered by an oxygen mask that made communication difficult. I prayed with him and assured him that I was there for him. Little did I know at the time that he would be gone in just a few short days.

Upon his death, I was asked to conduct Gary's funeral. I knew that he had accepted the Lord, so preaching his funeral wasn't necessarily as sad as it otherwise could have been. It was what happened afterward that would prove to be a little more nerve-racking.

At the conclusion of the service, I was approached by a young woman, who was a friend of Gary's daughter. Tears welled in her eyes as she told me about her own father's terminal illness. He had been fighting cancer for a very long time, and the sadness of the disease didn't come close to matching the heartache that she and her mother felt knowing beyond a shadow of a doubt that he was not ready with God; and time was running out. At the end of our conversation she told me that she had heard me preach once before and that time as well as the funeral message had convinced her that her father would listen to me. She felt that time was of the essence and asked if I would agree to meet with him. Of course, I agreed but I must admit in the days ahead as I became more informed of just what awaited me severe doubts came rushing in, and the eagerness to accept this *assignment* began to wane.

You see, this man had spent the majority of his sixty-seven years not only running from God but learning to hate or even tolerate anything related to God. Jehovah's Witnesses, as well as members of the Church of Latter-day Saints, didn't stand a chance with this guy!

He believed in equality to a certain extent as he would slam the door equally hard in their faces if they dared to show up at his residence. I know, because he told me so.

Relationships with some family members were not only strained but in tatters because of *Christianity*. Now this man was going to allow me into his home to show him the love of God and share the Gospel with him? I had my doubts, to say the least.

The appointed day arrived, and I believe it was a late Friday afternoon. I remember thinking as I rang the doorbell that if I could last fifteen minutes, then maybe I might have a chance to have the Holy Spirit give me something to say that would be so profound that he would at least consider it later. (Isn't it funny how we humans somehow limit the possibilities of the God that we routinely call "Almighty"?)

I took a deep breath as the door opened, and his daughter greeted me. She introduced me to her mother and said to have a seat in the living room, and she would go into the kitchen to get her father.

After a few moments, he entered the living room, and what I saw convinced me that his health situation was indeed dire. The ashen color of cancer had taken root in his skin. I stood up to shake his hand, and I remember introducing myself by saying that I had recently met his daughter, and she thought that I might be able to talk to him about something that was important to her and his wife.

It was at that time that he began to set the ground rules for our encounter, including the fact that he didn't expect me to be there very long.

He proceeded to put me on notice of my future fate by telling me about the various attempts that were made both recently and throughout the years to convince him to change his mind about God. Some of these encounters with those who dared to ring his door bell were random. Of these he somewhat gleefully told me that he took pleasure in shutting the door in their faces before they sometimes even got their greetings or tracks out. Some were family members who I would learn later had led to literally years of estrangement over their belief in God and Jesus Christ.

However, there was clearly something between him and his daughter that allowed him to tolerate this intrusion on one of the last days of his life. I was further intrigued later when he informed me that he had handcrafted a wooden nativity scene that he would erect every Christmas. There had to be something there, even when he was clearly relating his disdain for the very subject I was there to discuss with him.

Jesus teaches us in Luke 12:12 not to be concerned when we find ourselves in a situation where we may not have the words to address. He said, "For the Holy Spirit will teach you in that very hour what you ought to say."

It was nearing the five-minute mark, and I hadn't been able to say anything but "Hello, sir."

Then he began a statement I am sure today as I was then that was meant to be a goodbye.

After making it clear that he had no time for these intrusive messages meant to get him to realize that he was a sinner, he ended the statement by exclaiming that he hated *religion*.

Upon hearing those last words, the Holy Spirit rose up within me, and without even thinking, I blurted out that we had something in common. I too hated religion, but I had come here to talk to him about something else. I came to talk to him about a relationship. I believe that God had done everything not to have us conform to a religion but to enter into a relationship.

The next two words that proceeded out of his mouth were the ones that I could have only dreamed about just a few moments earlier. Looking at me, he simply said, "Go on," as he waved to me to have a seat. He struggled to make his way to the easy chair that had been set up to accommodate his current situation.

For the next hour and a half, I preached the Christmas tree effect—one majestic branch at a time. I assured him that I wasn't there to point out any sin that he may or may not have committed, except to prove to him that they had been forgiven. I was not there to preach to him about Satan or hell, except that he was defeated, and hell can be avoided. I related the fact that as many times as he may have been preached to about his unforgiven sin being a barrier that that message, as well as it may have been intended, was simply wrong.

The good news contained in the Gospel is simply this that God has *already* forgiven *all* our sins (Colossians 2:12) and thrown them into the sea (Micah 7:19).

I told him that not only has God remitted our sin, He has also promised to do something that not very many of us in the human race are capable of doing and that is *forgetting them* (Hebrews 8:12, 10:17).

Finally, I gave him a bit of my testimony to him telling him some of the unspeakable acts that I had previously committed because, after all, Revelation 12:11 (KJV) promises that "they overcame him by the blood of the Lamb, and by the word of their testimony." I felt that this situation definitely required some serious overcoming!

THE CHRISTMAS TREE EFFECT

I began to feel our time was drawing to a close because Raymond was getting visibly weaker. It was, at that moment, he said one of the last things he said to me literally gave me goose bumps.

With a mist in his eyes, he simply responded that he had done some very bad things in his life, and he always deep down inside hoped there was a god, like the one I described. It was the very reason that he never wanted to discuss the benefits of a god that the vast majority of the people whom He came in contact with described as angry and judgmental. I felt he was actually describing a scenario of "What's the use?"

Upon hearing this, the Holy Spirit welled up inside me and the words that tumbled from my mouth were simply not my own. It seemed that God had saved the best for last. It was now time to relate to this man perhaps the simplest and most perfect branch of the Christmas tree effect.

Leaning forward, I said, "You know, Peter received a revelation from God that he perceived God was not a respecter of persons (Acts 10:34, KJV). To me, this meant if He did it for me, He will do it for you. In fact, the beauty of the Gospel is that He already has. Your job is simply to accept it."

With that, I gave him an assignment. If anything I said to him that afternoon rang true or made some sense to him, I wanted him to promise me something. I reminded him that God had removed every barrier to a relationship with him by remitting his sin. It was now his move to repent.

Repenting is not groveling on the floor and pleading with God to forgive you or reminding Him just what a reprehensible person that you are; it is accepting what God has already done for you.

Romans 10:9 (KJV) told us, "That if thou shalt confess with thy mouth the Lord Jesus, and shalt believe in thine heart that God hath raised him from the dead, thou shalt be saved."

Notice there is nothing in that verse that requires begging for forgiveness. In fact, I truly believe receiving your salvation is even less complicated than this verse. I believe that salvation can be a one-word reply, just like the thief on the cross or the word that Saul uttered from the ground on which he had fallen, and that word is *Lord*!

Let me explain: the act of confessing His lordship *to* Jesus means you believe He *is* alive *and* God has indeed already raised Him from the dead. It is not recorded that Saul of Tarsus begged for mercy or forgiveness when he fell to the ground.

Upon hearing the voice of Jesus, he simply asked, "Who art thou Lord? Saul of Tarsus soon became Paul and was responsible for over one half of the New Testament. The thief on the cross only had to believe that God was *going* to raise Jesus from the dead to be invited by Jesus to join Him in paradise that very day. The fact of the matter is we have assimilated begging for forgiveness into the prerequisite for God to bestow salvation upon us. I am going to make this as uncomplicated as I can.

Repentance in the Bible is defined as "changing one's mind." It entails changing your mind that Jesus knows what is best for you instead of you. It is you allowing Him to drive the car instead of you grabbing the wheel.

With that, I arose and shook Raymond's hand and told him that I hoped to see him again, and he replied that he hoped so to.

Eight days later, I called his wife and asked if I could visit. Her voice had a tinge of hope in it. She said to come right over. The man that I met that afternoon was different. He was warmer and more welcoming. There was something else I noticed at the same time. He looked in much worse physical condition than I since I saw him last. There were also some friends and relatives visiting. God is so wonderful! He found a way that he and I could be alone for a just a stolen moment. I asked how he was doing, and it was then that I saw he had the same wonderment on his face that I had noticed when he first heard the Christmas tree effect. I will never forget his next words. He simply said that all was well and everything was taken care of. There was something else on his face that I was introduced to that day…a smile!

On July 9, 2012, Raymond's daughter called me to let me know that her father was near death and asked if I could visit. When I entered the living room, he was in his easy chair, unconscious. I whispered to him that I was there and said a prayer. He was on what appeared to be a morphine drip for comfort. Most of the immediate family was there, as well as a nurse from hospice.

After several hours, I decided to go home but directed Raymond's wife and daughter to call anytime they needed me.

Before leaving for work the next morning, after hearing nothing from the family, I called his daughter for an update. She said he was still holding on. I let her know I would stop by on my way to work. He was definitely still holding on, but the time between breaths was longer and his breathing was shallower.

After about a half hour, I again excused myself and asked that I wished to be called if his situation became even worse. Immediately upon getting to work, my cell phone rang, and I was informed that upon his daughter leaving the living room for the first time in over a day to see me out through the kitchen, Jesus had arranged transportation to escort Raymond to his new home. To this day, she contends that her father had waited until the moment she left the room to die because he didn't want her to witness his departure. Who could argue with her?

The day would not end without the family giving me one of the biggest honors of my life. I was asked to be the officiant at Raymond's funeral. It did feel like the fitting end of this whirlwind couple of weeks. There on the day of the funeral, I met Raymond's son and namesake before the funeral. He lived in Florida and recounted how he and his father's relationship had deteriorated throughout the years. In fact, the biggest falling out happened when his son had dared to become a Christian and attempted to witness to his father. I believe it was at that moment that I realized something my brother had tried to tell me years earlier after relaying my desire to *do big things for God*. He reminded me that very often, our definition of *big things* and God's can be very different. You see, the Bible stated, "I say unto you, that likewise joy shall be in heaven over *one* sinner that repenteth, more than over ninety and nine just persons, which need no repentance" (Luke 15:7, KJV). I had no doubt that the celebration in heaven over Raymond's decision had been an epic one!

The amazing intersection between Raymond and myself was not simply a *one-off* or the only example or confirmation of the preaching the Christmas tree effect. It was simply the first of many manifestations of it.

For the seven plus years since receiving this revelation, I have had the honor of preaching in a few different churches as a guest minister. In each one of them, a curious, wonderful phenomenon has emerged when I have given folks in the congregation the opportunity to give their life to Jesus. Many people who have been members of these congregations for many years have come forward. To say that I was both stunned and overjoyed would be quite the understatement. It seems that even after years of sitting, often times in the same seat or pew, they had heard nothing that had prompted them to make that decision in the past. The fact that this message at that time finally drove them to make the decision that they had been avoiding for years speaks volumes as to its effectiveness. Maybe that's what Jesus was trying to say with the parable of the lost sheep. Maybe, just maybe in every group of one hundred, there is that one who needs to hear just how much God loves them and how much they are missed and wanted in order to finally be found.

CHAPTER 10

The Star

On just about every Christmas tree, there is a focal point. It is a place or ornament that *shines* its attention to the tree. Usually this is at the very top. Now there are a few who may clip on a bird (usually a cardinal) or have a stylish St. Nicholas sitting atop their tree. However, I suspect that the majority of tree toppers remain the star. It can come in various styles. It can light up or not, but it is meant to draw the attention to the tree itself, the piece de resistance if you will.

I must admit that in putting this book to bed, I was struggling with what the star on the Christmas tree effect would represent. What would God put on the top of the tree to draw our attention to the beauty and majesty of the Gospel of Jesus Christ? It wasn't until a recent MercyMe concert that He revealed it to me.

Right there in the middle of the song "Grace Got You," the Holy Spirit rose up in my heart and literally said in my spirit, "There is the star—the grace of God." Of course it is. *Duh*, was my reaction. It is God's grace and mercy that made it possible for Jesus to utter the words "repentance and remission of sin." In fact, it is precisely the grace of God that was the prerequisite to the remission of sin. Without it, repentance would be a futile exercise.

What a dichotomy it is in today's churches where sin, judgment, and the wrath of God are the focus of their messages all the while singing songs of grace and mercy. In fact, my wife and I had noticed in the past couple of years while attending one of these churches of the overwhelming absence of these types of messages from either modern contemporary Christian songs or even the old beloved hymns of the church. In fact, I would dare anyone to find a song or hymn whose focus is the wrath and destruction that God *wants* to rain down upon His disobedient children at any moment. In fact, the opposite is true.

Of the many millions of songs and hymns written in the past two thousand or so years, none illustrates the star on the Christmas tree effect more than "Amazing Grace." This beloved hymn is almost two hundred fifty years old. It has over nine hundred seventy different arrangements and has been recorded over three thousand two hundred times. It is sung at all different settings from weddings, funerals, and church services all over the world an estimated ten million times *each year*. Why? The melody isn't particularly haunting or catchy. The words, though inspiring, are not even the amazing part of the hymn; it is the word itself and what it represents that is truly amazing. It is simply grace that is the star of this show, God's amazing grace!

How amazing is this grace?

For the past seven years, I have shared this message or parts thereof wherever and whenever I am asked to preach. It has never let me down and has always produced fruit sometimes providing stunning proof to its truth. Each time I prepare a message, the Christmas tree effect gets further refined by the Holy Spirit.

One thing that God has shown me time and time again is that the biggest revelations come from the smallest words. Words that are found in the Bible, such as *and*, *but*, and particularly *therefore*, can very often shed new light on old teaching. Perhaps, nowhere in the Bible is this point better illustrated than in Ephesians 2:1–5, which says,

> And you hath he quickened, who were dead in trespasses and sins; Wherein in time past ye walked according to the course of this world, according to the prince of the power of the air, the spirit that now worketh in the children of disobedience: Among whom also we all had our conversation in times past in the lusts of our flesh, fulfilling the desires of the flesh and of the mind; and were by nature the children of wrath, even as others. *But* God, who is rich in mercy, for his great love wherewith he loved us, Even when we were dead in sins, hath quickened us together with Christ (by grace ye are saved).

Take particular note of the word *but*. It is there to introduce a clause that will contradict the thought that has come before. In other words, Paul is telling the Ephesians that even when we were considered persona non grata, God still saved us through mercy and grace by Jesus Christ because of His great love.

I now feel the time has come to put this revelation of the Christmas tree effect into word form for others to read and use. God knows what He is doing. These verses in the Gospels have passed the test of time, and as our nation and the world get further polarized, the

THE CHRISTMAS TREE EFFECT

simplicity of God's Gospel is the perfect antidote for the increasing coldness and yes, even militancy seen in a lot of our churches today.

As I have previously written, Matthew records the prophesy of Jesus as it relates to the end times in the twenty-fourth chapter of his Gospel this way:

> And the love of the great body of people will grow cold because of the multiplied lawlessness *and* iniquity, but he who endures to the end will be saved. And this good news of the kingdom (the Gospel) will be preached throughout the whole world as a testimony to all the nations, and then will come the end. (Matthew 24:12–14, Amplified Bible, Classic Edition)

Proverbs 30:6 (KJV) states, "Add thou not unto his words, lest he reprove thee, and thou be found a liar." The danger of adding anything is that the original intent tends to be diluted the more that is added to it. The mission that Jesus Christ gave all of us those many years ago is really quite simple. We are to preach the Gospel everywhere to everyone. We have not been commissioned to be Lord. That job is still filled, and none of us are qualified for the position.

The Gospel is meant to be an introduction to Jesus Christ. This Gospel is five simple words. It is repentance and remission of sin (Luke 24:47). Adding any other meaning, particularly sin, only serves to build back up the wall that God sent His Son to tear down through the shedding of His blood at Calvary. It clutters the beauty of the Christmas tree that represents this Gospel. It diverts from the enormous love that the Father has toward us and is simply a lie. What lie? The lie we are told, or we tell ourselves that we must somehow measure up to what God expects of us in order to gain or earn His love and respect. What a cold slap in the face to the amazing grace that He has shown to us *first* that is.

Brennan Manning has always said it best. In almost every book he authored and in every message that he ever preached, he would remind us a simple and yet searing truth: "God loves you as you are and not as you should be because none of us is as we should be." Simple, right?

About the Author

Clark Dunkle was born, raised, and still lives in Carlisle, Pennsylvania, with his wife, Teresa. He has three grown-up children and three granddaughters. A graduate of Carlisle High School and Shippensburg University, Mr. Dunkle has spent the better part of his life as an administrator in the health care industry. He was called into the ministry in 2003. At the time, he was truly a broken man who felt like he would be the least likely candidate to receive a calling on his life. God's amazing grace intervened, and Mr. Dunkle has been an itinerant minister preaching to and assisting in pastoring small congregations in South Central Pennsylvania ever since.

In June of 2011, in a confluence of events that included the death of his mother and a diagnosis of prostate cancer, he received a revelation from God that changed his ministry to this day. It is a revelation that he calls the Christmas tree effect.